I0490841

The
Task At Hand

Markets, Organizations, And Strategy Should Be Centered On Consumer Demands.

By

James m. Diaz

Table of content

Introduction

Introduction to The Task At Hand One of the fundamental tenets of TTAH is that customers are not always seeking a specific product, but rather a solution to a problem or difficulty that they are facing is one of the fundamental tenets of TTAH.

To create solutions that effectively "solve" the task that the consumer is seeking to complete, businesses must comprehend the underlying wants and motivations of their customers. Practically speaking, adopting TTAH in product development entails the following essential steps:

1. **Determine the task that the client is attempting to complete:** Understanding the precise goal or difficulty that the client is attempting to solve is the first step. Getting insights into customers' wants and motives may entail performing market research, participating in customer interviews, or analyzing consumer data.

2. **Test and verify the solution**: Before the introduction of the product or service, it is crucial to test and validate the solution to make sure it satisfactorily addresses the demands and solves the customer's problem. To obtain feedback and make any required changes to the product or service, this

may entail carrying out user testing, pilot projects, or other types of market research.

In general, employing TTAH in product development necessitates a thorough comprehension of consumer behavior and the underlying demands and motives that shape it.

Companies may create solutions that better fulfill the demands of their consumers and promote business success by concentrating on the task that the client is attempting to do rather than the product itself. Please hit the "purchase button" right away if you are interested in the task at hand.

CHAPTER 1

How does Work To Be Done work?

There has been a lot of debate among innovators about Jobs to Be Done (JTBD) and for good reason. It makes sense that this theory would spark so much discussion because, like other hypotheses, it was tried, modified, and adjusted before taking on its current form. JTBD has been impacted by a number of theories and tenets from the management and psychology sectors. It makes sense why some people could disagree on certain details. So that you can benefit the most from the "tasks to be done idea, our objective in this post is to concentrate on the most pertinent information about it.

The guiding principles of Jobs To Be Done

The Tasks to be Done is a sophisticated theoretical framework that gets even more so when seen from many aspects. Theodore Levitt's renowned adage, "People don't want a quarter-inch drill, they want a quarter-inch hole," is one of the simplest ways to illustrate JTBD theory. This is evident in our daily lives and surroundings. We purchase goods or services to complete tasks, meet needs, or complete jobs. We either purchase a drill or hire someone to make the hole in the wall. In the end, it all comes down to the advancement we want to make and the result. But more on that in the paragraphs that follow. Returning to the foundational idea around which the Jobs to Be Done theory has been developed, let's now. They serve as a launching pad for pursuing innovation using the Jobs to be Done methodology. But, it's also important to keep in mind that the JTBD theory has its flaws and cannot be applied to every innovation project you can think of. It is not a panacea.

1. Goods and services are used to advance. You need to consider their future goals, as well as the surrounding conditions, in order to comprehend why people choose to use or purchase particular things. When people use services and products to advance, they have value.

2. A job is reliable and enduring. The fundamental task remains the same, even though products and services may come and go. Consumers merely choose to resign from the old product and hire a new one that does the task more effectively.

3. JTBD's three dimensions, Careers have social, emotional, and functional aspects that a solution can address all at once.

4. JTBD's three tiers. Find the job, make the needed experiences, and then integrate them around the job. As a result, you will have a competitive advantage because you can solve problems that others can't.

5. The source of competitive advantage is processing. Procedures must be streamlined for advancement, coordinated, and in line with a compelling customer's job.

6. List the most important metrics.

7. JTBD can be used in all types of organizations and fields. Different teams can employ the idea because it offers a methodical approach to comprehending people's motivators.

What are the advantages of Jobs To Be Done and why is it important?

JTBD theory implementation takes time. By developing and using flexible procedures, organizations must gradually move toward a jobs-centric strategy while also measuring the appropriate metrics. It's not simple, but it's worth the effort to make sure that every important decision made within an **organization**—from product development to marketing and **customer service**—is informed by the needs of the consumer. Here are a few advantages you might enjoy along the way.

1. Recognize how demand is generated

Christensen expands The Tasks to Be Done Theory to incorporate the forces in "Competing Against Luck.", and. According to this, you need to entice buyers away from competitive products in order to generate demand. Many businesses make the mistake of assuming that substantial changes to a solution are sufficient to persuade clients to switch. Organizations should investigate what prompts clients to switch solutions since the work itself does not change. Later in this article, we will talk more about the forces of advancement.

2. It changes your point of view and aids in redefining your company.

With this new strategy, you can identify customers where none previously existed and opportunities where issues once existed.

For instance, you could presume that Netflix's competitors are other streaming services like Disney, HBO, or Amazon Prime when you think of them. Netflix, on the other hand, was highly aware of the tasks that their clients need, and they strived to complete them. Video games, nights out with friends, outdoor games, and other forms of amusement are also rivals when their clients are looking for entertainment.

3 Long-term advantage in the market

Effective job-based inventions are challenging to replicate because they pay attention to both the "big hire," or when the purchase is made, and the "small hire," or when the customer first uses the product. Job-based innovations are challenging to replicate because of the level of detail at these touch points. Based on their post-purchase experiences, consumers choose which products are superior to others.

4 Promotes independence and creativity

Organizations that put a priority on the job enable people to make clear decisions. Tasks to be Done can serve as focal points for employees; hence, the more thoroughly they comprehend the problems they resolve, the simpler it will be for them to make wise choices and exercise autonomy and creativity.

5. Allow for lean operations

When the organization's objectives are centered on the job, waste, costs, and time are all but eliminated. Because it's simpler to allocate human resources in accordance with procedures and priorities once everyone is aware of the progress a customer is trying to achieve, the influence on productivity may also be significant.

JTBD: When and When to Use

It's crucial to initially put in the effort to determine the precise jobs that your consumers need to perform, regardless of where or how you want to use Jobs to spur greater innovation.

What additional contexts can JTBD be used in?

6 Message and Placement

It makes a big difference in how you present the value you offer to customers and how you position your goods and services. You run the risk of being employed for the wrong reasons if you improperly convey your offer and your case for hiring you. When this occurs, it is virtually hard to avoid disappointing someone. Businesses like Uber, Google, Disney, LinkedIn, and others have developed "purpose brands" as a result of their names becoming a reflection of the tasks you can complete with their assistance. They succeed by doing a job effectively and clearly communicating the problem they solve.

Don't forget to center your messaging on the jobs rather than the goods. How much do we typically value a feature of a product? Indeed, we're interested in the advancements such features will allow us to make.

7 Client development

Based on factors like gender, age, wealth, and other factors, demographic segmentation doesn't tell much about client demands. The majority of marketers have relied on this time-tested technique, sometimes referred to as "buyer persona creation," to pinpoint the demographics most likely to purchase your goods or services. They occasionally also take into account client behavior, but frequently these methods are constrictive and don't reveal the genuine wants or the reasons why customers select a particular solution.

With JTBD, you may develop a needs-based segmentation that can aid in identifying new prospects, market gaps, and consumer challenges.

You can develop a needs-based segmentation with Jobs to be Done that can help you comprehend consumer problems, market gaps, or new business opportunities.

Job To Be Done implementation in easy steps

Before starting started with JTBD, it's important to note that this theory, technique, or process has its limitations and boundaries, just like every other theory, method, or process out there. It can be difficult to identify and define the appropriate tasks that explain why your company exists. Even though it is about the advancement that the customers want to make, this does not imply that every incentive is necessarily a task that has to be completed.

So, how do you begin? Set your goals, what you want to accomplish, and how much time and resources you are willing to commit as a first step. Given that this is a lengthy You must endeavor to prepare both yourself and your organization for change.

It's crucial to be deliberate in your JTBD efforts and to inform everyone of what will happen next, their responsibility, the various ways they can participate, etc. If you're interested in learning more about how to announce the start of a new project, check out the article we created on the subject, which also includes some helpful templates. The initial phases involve increasing awareness and trust. Be ready to allay the anxieties and concerns without brushing them aside because you can anticipate some pushback. Start small with individual JTBD projects that can be a success story the organization wants to duplicate and scale, so as not to become discouraged. After you have a plan in place, take these three

significant actions:

Chapter 2

Understand the customer's job

Consumers are at the center of the JTBD idea, and getting to know them better can help you understand their needs—or what we now refer to as the "Jobs"—better. Interviews are crucial when using Jobs theory because they reveal patterns and motivations that were previously hidden.

Selecting the consumers you'll speak with based on predetermined criteria, such as those who have recently purchased your product, those who have left you for the competition, or those who have been a part of your business the longest, is the first stage in conducting the interviews. You can use these factors to shorten the list of candidates you need to interview. Take your time developing and analyzing the material you gather because interviews are an important step in understanding the jobs. An interview should span at least 30 minutes and cover all facets of the position, including the social, functional, and emotional facets. While having a well-thought-out plan is a fantastic place to start, understanding what questions to ask and how is essential.

Indirectly and with open-ended questions, inquire about behaviors, hiring standards, rewards, and motivators. Even while it's best to establish a plan and a strategy, it's also beneficial to wander off track briefly and see where things are heading in conversations. Discussions should flow naturally. You'll remember all you want to cover in your interview if you take notes and prepare ahead of time. Our full Tasks To Be Done package, which also offers further advice, templates for interview questions, scripts, and invitation emails, was created to assist you with this process.

2. Job Mapping

Start information mapping and analysis once the interviews are over. Finding the proper work depends a lot on how you put the puzzle pieces together. Ideally, you start noticing certain patterns, such as common experiences, reoccurring behaviors, avenues utilized to find new answers, selection criteria they take into account, and worries or phobias associated with what prevented them from making a particular option. Don't ignore crucial details about your rivals and eliminate the words and phrases used to characterize them. After completing this stage, you should have conducted at least a few interviews with a significant number of repeatable responses.

You might find multiple jobs, thus you should rank them in order of importance depending on which ones offer greater opportunities. We go into greater detail on the tools that will aid you in completing this stage in the section that follows.

Work on the solution. By this point, you ought to have determined the task or tasks that your clients must complete. With all of this information at your disposal, you ought to be prepared to begin creating a solution or enhancing the one that already exists.

Your response should address their motivation and take into account the emotional, social, and functional factors that characterize the development they are looking for now that you are aware of what they are looking for. Your proposed solution must be as intricate as the task at hand. Having established all the intricacies of the assignment will help create a roadmap for the solution. Ranking by outlining every detail of a task, you can develop a blueprint for the answer that you can use as a practical guide for innovation.

Until addressing the big "why," don't begin to improve your goods or services. Why would customers choose your updated or new products, and what influences their choices? It is advisable to combine everything into a narrative rather than split the information up into discrete information clusters. Storyboarding enables you to situate the development inside a context and on a timeframe. Build on the social, emotional, and functional components of your customer's employment by

putting them all together using the
interviewer's responses.

CHAPTER 3

Tools and methods to apply Jobs to be Done

The authors of "Competing against luck" do not recommend any particular tool or technique for doing JTBD. Instead, they place a strong emphasis on the necessity of knowing what a job is and isn't, as well as the importance of supporting systems.

It's crucial to first grasp the fundamentals, even though there could be minor variations in how they construct the theory. This makes it simpler to combine and match the tools and resources that will assist you in identifying Tasks to Be Done, implementing them across your business, and fusing this with additional research and innovation-fostering techniques.

1. **The Job map**

A client's goals are reflected in a job map, which is distinct from a process map or a customer journey experience. The eight steps on the job map outline what customers are attempting to accomplish.

This tool enables you to identify all the areas in which a client might require assistance or support.

All work can be broken down into these eight processes, which should make it simpler for businesses to find more chances for innovation and differentiation. Instead of focusing on what or how customers are currently doing something, the objective is to determine what they want to achieve at each stage.

1. Specify - What details of the work need to be specified by the

customer in order to move forward? Look at ways to make consumers' planning simpler and to assist them to grasp their goals.

2. **Find** - the inputs that must be found in order to complete the task.

3. **How can the inputs be ready for the task?** You can consider ways to organize, automate, and make the setup process simpler in this step.

4. **Confirm** - Verifying that the planning was accurate and confirming readiness.

5. **Carry out** - What must be done to carry out the task successfully? Consider how you may assist customers by giving them feedback in real-time or by making sure the execution is accurate.

6 What needs to be monitored in order to support the execution? This is crucial since the execution may require modifications. Systems that enable precise and automatic monitoring are extremely valuable.

1. **Modify** — Customers may occasionally need assistance

updating, changing, or amending the job. They may want assistance in determining not only what needs altering, but also when and how.

2. **Conclusion** - this shouldn't be misconstrued because even if the task is coming to a close, it isn't any less significant. If the task at hand is cyclical, you might be able to find a way to contribute to a successful transition from one cycle to the next.

The job map can be utilized as a framework for projecting and comprehending future growth as well

as a roadmap for job discovery interviews.

 The Pull forces (moving away from an old solution to a new one) - The difficulties or constraints with a present solution - They may be drawn to something new, other advantages, or they may be early adopters.

• Push factors (what makes customers stick to their old solution and what pushes them away from you)
- Force of habit - using the outdated methods

- Aversion to change and anxiety in the face of uncertainty

Plan your interviews with the forces of advancement in mind.

Planning based on the discovery

Simply put, discovery-driven planning is a method for creating new businesses that are less risky.

For a strategy to work, it must be validated.

The steps in discovery-driven planning are as follows:

1. Clearly define what success means to you in terms of specifics. You

make a reverse income statement at this stage.

2. Use benchmarks to determine whether your idea is feasible.

3. Specify the operational needs. Be critical of what it takes to achieve the goals as you lay out the resources that are needed.

4. List your presumptions. Describe each supposition used in your estimates of profits, revenues, and expenses.

5. Make plans based on important checkpoints. Plan out your strategy

and add checkpoints to see if your presumptions are accurate or if they need to be revised.

With discovery-driven planning, you must be willing to accept that you will frequently be proven wrong and be at ease with repeatedly changing your assumptions and checkpoints.

Employment Best Practices

When implemented properly, JTBD may be a potent tool for fostering creativity within your company, but in order to execute it well, the relevant jobs must be identified. We selected the top three best practices that are really effective.

1. Let the reality around you inspire you Several of the most popular items have resulted from individual tasks. Market research is crucial, but occasionally we overlook the obvious areas to explore. Observe and look for opportunities in the things others try to do or in their problems, whether it's in your own life or in someone else's.

What coping mechanisms or compensatory behaviors do they exhibit? Sometimes someone is dissatisfied with the options for a problem they want to fix. In this manner, ING Direct was created.

A parent devised a do-it-yourself method to educate his son on the importance of saving and budgeting. Ln response, ING Direct launched an online bank service that included savings accounts, mutual funds, and certificates of deposit. They talked about Creating neighborhood offices in the shape of cafes allowed consumers to interact with the bank while addressing emotional factors like a lack of trust or apprehension about change.

1. Examine how users of your product behave.

Unusual applications for specific items offer tremendous opportunities. Consider the case of baking soda. Arm & Hammer saw an opportunity in the new chores that needed to be done when their research revealed that customers were using baking soda as laundry detergent, toothpaste mix, carpet cleaners, or odor absorbents. As a result of their research, the company created new products that addressed those particular tasks and adopted a new marketing approach to promoting all the applications for the product.

3. Understand what is a job and what is not

One easy trick for this is to keep in mind that adjectives or adverbs usually don't depict genuine occupations. Instead, a more abstract definition of a real job is used. Another piece of advice is that it's not solving for a job if the solution to your issue falls under the same category of goods.

You are limited to only offering other drinks that are similar when someone requests a milkshake. Completely different categories of goods may provide the answer if someone claims they need to keep busy on the way to work in order to avoid being hungry for a few hours.

1. Selecting the incorrect rivals

As was already mentioned, you can be thinking about competition incorrectly if you just consider goods or services in the same category. As we've already shown, JTBD theory isn't exactly connected to any one good or service; rather, it's about the progress people wish to make. The identical task can be completed with goods from entirely other categories.

Consider what clients would discontinue utilizing or purchasing if they opted for your solution. In this manner, you can keep from coming up with a useless solution. Do study outside of your industry and search for rivals in less visible areas.

2 Use of incorrect data

Data can quickly become a double-edged sword. Due to the widespread belief that quantitative data is the only unbiased source of factual information, market research has traditionally focused on it. (what transpires after the buy, when, and how they utilize a solution).

Pay equal attention to qualitative data, such as observations and insights that typically don't fit in a spreadsheet, to prevent this.

1. **Waiving job-related emphasis**

Companies begin to expand once they recognize a crucial task and figure out how to do it. That's when people are dragged into the "growth temptation" and start losing focus on the task that made everything happen. This results in a desire to increase sales, grow, and reach more clients.

Trying to find solutions for numerous clients and jobs at once might, however, backfire. Even while concentrating on one task and executing it effectively is difficult, it's what helped so many organizations prosper. Always ask yourself: Are you only concerned with promoting expansion, or are you also taking into account the advancements that clients are attempting to achieve in their lives?

Give the problem you're fixing a voice and a champion to keep your attention on it. Effective management stops daily organizational methods from deviating from your initial task. Processes for a job-centric organization must be created around the job and integrated into the culture.

1. **A vague job**

If you can't be clear and describe the job, you could fall into the trap of offering a solution that works for everyone, and that usually fails. You must take organizing around that job into account if you choose to employ the Jobs theory as one of the strategies to promote more creativity.

Focusing on the task at hand or explaining it to everyone in the organization is not something that comes easily. However, It's a crucial stage, and how you convey change and

how everyone is contributing much
depends on the organizational culture

CHAPTER 4

3 TIPS FOR UNDERSTANDING AND APPLYING THE JOBS TO BE DONE THEORY

1. **Take note**

Without observing people, it is impossible to find work to be done. For the purpose of identifying and validating the tasks to be performed, extensive market research, including consumer interviews and observation, is required. You can only completely understand the functional, social, and emotional "jobs" that your product or services can fulfill by paying attention to consumer actions.

Chris Larson, a former Disruptive Strategy participant, considers the personal experiences that improved his comprehension of the jobs-to-be-done notion.

My mother was doing cosmetics while she was driving and talking on the phone when I finally got my "ah-ha" moment, according to Larson. "How might I make this simpler and safer, I wondered in my brain. Then I made the crucial connection by asking, "What was the task at hand here?

Larson's experience reveals a fundamental component of the JTBD hypothesis. Instead of developing a JTBD after having a concept for a product or service, you can find out what jobs someone needs a product or service for by watching how people behave.

1. **Put the job first and the product second.**

As you become aware of JTBD in your daily life, it can be tempting to focus right away on the goods or services that can meet those needs. JTBD isn't, however, about the product; that comes after. However, it's crucial to concentrate on the task at hand rather than the end result as you become more adept at applying the theory in practical settings.

You risk missing the wider picture by being too preoccupied with creating the final result. What position are you looking for? Once the appropriate work is found, the product will appear. The most difficult aspect is that.

1. **The procedure**

Understanding and applying the JTBD theory is a process. You must first comprehend the theory. Case studies and examining instances of JTBD in action are excellent resources for establishing that base. Yet you need a strategic mindset to put the theory into practice and inspire fresh, original ideas.

examples of to-be-completed tasks

By assisting consumers in completing their Tasks to be Done, successful companies respond to their demands. Below are a few examples of products and businesses that fit the JTBD philosophy.

Consider this in cases where some of these businesses or goods are not as popular as they once were: What has changed—the product, the job, or the client's requirements and expectations? How can a business successfully finish one Job while making a shift when the environment does?

Tasks to Complete Example 1:

"I need a phone that will let me listen to music as I run." Customer feedback The Sony Walkman and Apple's iPod are two significant devices that address This Work to be Done. Both of these items represented significant advancements in the ability to listen to music on the go, providing the consumer with more options than just choosing a radio station.

The iPod utilizes modern technologies and satisfies user expectations regarding the portability of music, whereas the

Walkman is fundamentally responding to the same Task to be Done.

Tasks to Be Done Example 2:

"I want to swiftly and simply shop for the book I want." Customer feedback It's nearly difficult to recall that Amazon once exclusively sold books. In those early years, Amazon provided a solution to the book availability issue for its customers. A brick-and-mortar business could only stock a certain number of different books, whereas Amazon could access a considerably wider selection. Despite the fact that

Amazon has grown to include numerous divisions and businesses, its core value of having a broad selection readily available still dominates all of its operations.

Tasks to Complete Example 3:

"I want to shop for books in a friendly setting where I can speak with knowledgeable people who share my interests." Customer feedback

What they don't provide is a setting that invites bookworms and readers into a physical location. That is why, even in a world with a website like Amazon, concrete bookstores still exist (although with a smaller capacity). Local bookshops offer a personalized touch that an online merchant like Amazon simply cannot match.

While some customers enjoy browsing the shelves and discussing new publications with the staff, physical bookshops continue to operate. This is particularly a website could never hope to duplicate, the bookstores that remain in operation offer an experience that addresses a Job to be Done.

 accurate for customers who frequent smaller, independent bookstores. Although these are

Tasks to Be Done Example 4:

"I want to get in touch with my classmates (and find out who is single)." Customer feedback

1. Whatever your opinions of social media in general and Facebook in particular, you cannot dispute how pervasive they have become in many users' lives today. While code and algorithms may be complex, the JTBD that Facebook completes

is remarkably straightforward compared to the JTBD that physical bookstores complete: the site facilitates user connections. Facebook, which was once only accessible to college students, is today utilized by millions of users worldwide.

Social animals include humans. Most of us yearn for some level of attention and connection. Speaking with your consumers directly about their objectives and difficulties will help you better comprehend their Tasks to be

Done. When clients understand that we are trying to meet their needs and how they function, they are frequently very open with their feedback.

The jobs-to-be-done hypothesis

To better company outcomes, marketers, decision-makers, and product developers must be aware of the occupations that occur in the lives of our customers. We must offer answers. The incorrect analytical unit is understanding who these people are. What they are trying to accomplish is what we truly want to know.

The "job" is a basic issue that a client must address in a certain circumstance at the core of the philosophy. We are pushed by the Jobs to be Done Theory to comprehend the client experience. Why do customers choose us over our competitors? Is it a result of our product's superior specifications? Are we the least expensive? is it? because of our excellent marketing division?

Three presumptions form the basis of the Jobs to be Done theory.

When you choose to use a Jobs to be Done strategy, you consent to make decisions based on a few basic presumptions.

1. Consumers purchase a good or service to carry out a particular duty.

A passenger wants to get somewhere, not just take a ride in a cab. A construction worker wants to carry materials from one location to another, not push a wheelbarrow.

A straightforward way to track hourly pay is what a payroll professional needs—not computer software.

Such a task turns into an assignment.

1. Strategies and innovations revolve around the task.

Products

As a result, if the customer's wants are consistently considered as the JTBD, they last longer and remain stable. On outcome-driven innovation, businesses can keep their attention.

1. The work that your clients do gives you entirely fresh viewpoints.

JTBD makes it possible for strategy, disruptive innovation, and product development to be based on consistent consumer needs that have the most potential for value generation. To better serve our customers, we ask for their opinions. We invest in creating solutions with real market value because we consider the Job to Be Done.

Why Is the Principle of Jobs to Be Done Important?

The Tasks to Be Done theory has various applications and can benefit your business in a variety of ways. Think of the following application areas, for instance:

• Customer centricity - Developing a team-wide understanding of customers and their demands.

• Consumer Segmentation - By requesting the various jobs, JTBD can act as the foundation for a new type of segmentation.

• Marketing - By highlighting pertinent product aspects, for instance, consumer approaches might be more pertinent.

• Competitive intelligence - JTBD may offer a unique viewpoint on the industry and the competitive environment.

• Innovation - JTBD gives you the ability to create new goods and business models that are more suited to meet all of the needs of the clientele.

How Can You Utilize Do It Yourself Jobs?

One of the firms that developed and pioneered the Jobs to be Done methodology, Strategy, an innovation consulting firm, reported that their inventive strategy had an 86% success rate compared to the average success rate of traditional innovation methods, which was 17%. Undoubtedly, a targeted innovation strategy approach outperforms the majority of ideation/chance-based techniques. Jobs Theory and the Jobs to be Done practices can be helpful tools for coming up with fresh concepts and creating ground-breaking products that enhance the value proposition of your company. And the basis of an agreement that will aid you in using the technique. The best way to execute it is through a workshop.

Consider the purposes for which customers utilize your product and the

jobs they hope to accomplish with it.
Think about the emotional and social
aspects in addition to the functional
ones. Each participant writes one need
on a moderation card to represent their
opinions.

The actions listed below give you

Review responses

Gather the solutions so that each
developer can briefly describe them. Put
related concepts under a single heading.
In addition, you have the option of
grouping by necessity (emotional,
functional, social).

convert objectives into user stories

Formulate both direct and indirect goals as user stories, such as "I buy the product too."

There should be a user story for each objective.

Why not?

Consider the reasons why customers don't purchase your goods as well as any substitutes, rivals, or workarounds that they might employ. Consider the objectives and goals of the customer when evaluating your product and alternatives.

Identify areas for development

To find areas where your strategy, product, or service needs to be improved, use the previous steps. Create hypotheses to better serve client demands, and specify metrics to monitor them.

Success talk

Speak with both clients and no clients. Consider both "why" and "why not" in your inquiries. If applicable, observe customers using your prototype or product. Test the hypothesis using the discussions and observations.

Businesses Need Work Argument
Going through all the hassles is
pointless if we merely use the
information to base unsupported, maybe
biased assumptions about the customer
on our own gut instincts. This is why
we advocate setting aside the necessary
capital to include the customers in your
business in a qualitative and
quantitative approach.

More investment security is desperately
needed for innovation. Emerging
corporate and private inventions fail
70% of the time, according to the most

upbeat figures, while 96% of them fail within the first year of their initial four-year lifespan. Only a small percentage of the survivors succeed. The majority of advances are still modest and unimportant to the broader market. The main cause of these startling figures is that not enough effort is being made to fully comprehend the wants of the consumer. Instead of considering customers' jobs, firms push technologies ahead blindly.

How Does The JTBD Framework Work?

Our propensity to interpret and comprehend the universe solely from the perspective of the business is the number one obstacle to innovation. In order to involve the customer in our dialogues and decision-making, we lack the framework and mental models. This is impossible, as evidenced by the fact that the majority of innovation ventures fail.

A thorough grasp of, among other things, what "tasks to accomplish" a customer has is the core of the Jobs to be Done paradigm for providing value. r has in particular life circumstances, how he or she chooses between options, what trade-offs are made, whether the "suffering" is severe enough that solutions are pieced together, and what factors influence the decision to choose an alternative. The JTBD Theory is built on the tenet that customers "commission" goods and services that enable them to accomplish goals and advance in their life. More significant innovations can be created the better one understands the job at hand and the decision-making procedure leading up to "commissioning" a solution. But, this approach is useful for more than just making strategic choices. Even the debate over which product features and functions to create (and which ones to leave out) may be very contentious. when there is an understanding of the jobs a client wants to be done, clarity in specific life situations, and how he or she makes decisions about alternatives.

Related: With the Business Model Canvas, what Does Customer Relationships Mean?

Giving the company a clear mission

In conclusion, the Tasks to be Done
Hypothesis provides a fresh perspective
on customers and their demands. It can
be employed to align the entire business
with what customers require, in addition
to serving as a guide for decisions
regarding specific products or product
strategies. The entire business and all of
its operations are aligned with the
customer in a way that is highly
relevant to the customer, as opposed to
having lofty, ambitious vision and
purpose statements. The activities at
hand act as a "North Star" that can

provide the business with a distinct, customer-focused purpose.

Summary of Tasks to Be Completed

JTBD

Jobs to be done is still a young idea or approach that does not ask about the characteristics of clients, but about the higher-level tasks (jobs) they wish to do.

This results in a fresh viewpoint on the product, the user, and the competitor. The strategy works best when supplemented with tried-and-true techniques, such as those from design thinking.

Questions and Answers

....

The primary issue that a client must fix in a specific circumstance.

How do you write your clients' Tasks to be Done?

Create a solid foundation through your customer's testing and outreach. Focus on the tasks that must be completed to satisfy your clients rather than developing ideas for new solutions. Keep the job description straightforward and limited to its essential components.

www.ingramcontent.com/pod-product-compliance
Lightning Source LLC
Chambersburg PA
CBHW071139220526
45467CB00015B/1520